3-8-54

The Businessman Must Save Himself

THE BUSINESSMAN MUST SAVE HIMSELF

BY W. H. McCOMB

HARPER & BROTHERS   Publishers   New York

Library of Congress catalog card number: 53-11852

DEDICATED TO ROGER W. BABSON

Who for over forty years has preached the essential message of this book to his clients, readers and the students of his three colleges: Babson Institute, Webber College and Utopia College

Contents

Contents

Preface

To the businessman the economic fallacies of communism always must seem obvious and the bright dreams of all shades of pink only an extension of the same absurdity. A chief purpose of this book is to show that this world Revolt of the Left advances only when equally absurd sins of business make it possible.

It is those sins of the businessman which have made depressions chronic; and in this world conflict of Left and Right it seems possible that another depression might be his last. It can happen here because it is happening now.

In this businessman's war for survival which rages coldly, his weaknesses appear to be the same which preceded the downfall of all those business freedoms of the past. From Carthage to England, he was always too busy making money to wield the power of money with the statesmanship which all power demands.

It was a life-long devotion to this literature of business, stimulated by his own modest financial commitments and supplementing observations as a newspaper writer in the United States, Latin America and Europe, which gave the author the audacity to offer to the businessman this new battle plan. It asserts that the real issue is not communism; that the real stake is the fate and future of the free businessman; and what must be necessary to save him is nothing less than a historic reformation in his own house.

W. H. M.

Miami, Florida
July 4, 1953.

The Businessman Must Save Himself

The Businessman Next Door

1

The Businessman Is on Trial

The businessman is on trial for his life. According to the prosecutor, he is responsible for our economic woes. He is accused as the exploiter of labor; the war monger who owns the munitions trust; the manipulator of phony stocks; the loan shark who fleeces widows and orphans; the briber of corrupt politicians, and the saboteur of American democracy. He is said to be the profiteer in war, the creator of depressions in peace, the inevitable enemy of all that is hopeful for a better world!

Such is the indictment by his enemies whose political complexions may range from campus rose to Moscow scarlet. In about one-third of the world, the defendant has been declared guilty. Tough fellows haul him into people's courts and then to slave labor camps. The businessmen of China now are finding this out.

THE BUSINESSMAN MUST SAVE HIMSELF

Here in America, the businessman has been given another chance. A "businessman's cabinet" has been handed the job of meeting the bill collector for the most gigantic debt that ever burdened man. His friends hope that no harm may come to business and the stock market.

In America the indictment contains another charge. The businessman has been accused of being a Babbitt. As such, he would be ridiculous if he didn't have the power of his money. The masses are taught that his concept of the civilized life is bigger bath tubs; his understanding is in the profit motive and his aspiration is to get the money. They are told that "in that empty but grasping brain of his," there is no understanding of the dreams of the poet and not even much sympathy for the hopes of the rest of us. What we want is peace and honesty and a decent living; but even a President has called the businessman an "economic royalist."

It is charged that he is so stupidly selfish that he has been blind to his own best interests, that his self-centered ignorance could pull down the civilization around us. Such fears are expressed by the "liberals" and "progressives" as they vacillate on the Near Left. With the outright communists there are no hesitations. To them the businessman is the wicked bourgeois, that word which in communist terms means Public Enemy No. 1.

In America the businessman has been viewed for years as a suspicious character. His mistakes were laid bare by the "muckraker." Then Sinclair Lewis exposed him as a fatuous oaf. After 1929 revealed to all the extent of his "wickedness," the New Dealers visited upon him the public wrath. They heaped taxes upon the fellow, sent officials to look over his books and piled on him questionnaires to fill out.

If anybody wants to go into the evidence, it has been dredged up to form mountains of literature. There are Gustavus Meyers' *History of the Great American Fortunes* and Lundberg's *America's Sixty Families.* There are the works of that whole generation of "muckrakers" about the sins of the "robber barons." With the dawn of the red millennium in Russia, the left-wing program became one of action, with a new generation of writers who dared to glorify the party line. Their works were supplemented on the higher levels by thick volumes from leftish professors of economics and sociology about how the businessman failed. These were greeted with some benediction in the Sunday book sections, the 25-cent magazines, and the "intellectual" weeklies. Even Joseph E. Davies in his *Mission to Moscow* could see hope in the red dawn.

It has been a long time since genuine praise has been given to the businessman. Elbert Hubbard and Ida Tarbell endeavored to defend him; but in literary circles their point of view is now as antiquated as Horatio Alger. After them our daring young men on the literary trapeze swarmed to the Left.

From the campus came a stream of volumes to show that capitalism was "disintegrating," that free competition of American business was "out-dated," and the hope of the sophomores had to be in the collectivist dawn. This "intellectual" trend against the businessman now has gone so far that it might even be difficult for a regiment of Ivy Lees to make him smell good.

If a "businessman's cabinet" should bring forth or even fail to prevent such a business holocaust as the businessman was charged with in the last Republican government, then he will be in worse odor than ever. If he is to exult over another chance, he might remember that his victory puts him squarely in front of the jury in this world-wide trial for his life. That chance might even be his last.

One thing that makes the position of the businessman so weak is that he himself seems to be so inarticulate. Since 1929 he has even seemed to suffer from a guilty conscience. He does not make a good job of defending himself in his own newspapers. He has the best-paid lawyers on his side, but they seem to be tongue-tied in the court of public opinion. In that ideological conflict between Left and Right now raging everywhere, they do not even seem to know their way around.

There are some businessmen whose only idea of defense is the slush fund, the subsidized newspaper, the bought vote. They have not yet learned that such armament is out-dated. Because they feel certain that their political adversary is a fraud, they feel that they must be bigger frauds to win.

It is true that any defense counsel for the businessman must encounter a serious difficulty. So many of the charges against him are true. The capitalists and tradesmen of this world have piled up an appalling record of offenses. Taken in bulk or detail, the charges make a formidable indictment even if the broader picture may be untrue. When the great day comes in the people's supreme court, the businessman may need a Clarence Darrow to defend him.

Darrow saved some culprits whose plight appeared just as desperate. If Darrow had the case, we might expect a revolutionary change in the businessman's defense tactics. We might expect to hear Darrow roar:

"Sure the businessman is guilty of a lot of things. Who isn't? In the infinite processes of building this world of ours, a lot of things have slipped. I file a warning. Before you turn this defendant over to the commissars, I want to remind you of what he has been building while the rest of us were talking; and I have a few words to say about those pink punks who want to take over the business."

It is the red—and also pink—challenge that the businessman is an evil character because he seeks profit. They charge that he has too much power in his money. They propose to take that power away from him and give it to the politico. They believe that the politico will be a more trustworthy character—especially if he reads Marx.

2

The Hidden Revolution

What the devil must like most to hear is babies crying in the dark for milk when there isn't any. What the devil must like most to see is their tormented papas cowering under police clubs when they try to get some milk. Americans have almost forgotten that such acute poverty exists.

Such suffering has been common ever since there have been men on this planet and it is still common in most of the world. A UNESCO report says that 1,400,000,000 persons—about two-thirds of the population of this world—are suffering from malnutrition.

How cruel this struggle for existence can be is not clearly realized by most Americans. Only those who have been outside of their own country can visualize famine in India and China, the squalor of Haiti or Honduras or the running sores in the streets of Egypt or Tunis, the brutal tyrannies of dictatorships and fake democracies or even the austerity of England. In Russia there was apparently a planned and man-made famine in which several millions of men, women and children were starved. Such crime staggers the American imagination. It was wholesale economic murder. In most of the world it is going on all the time at retail.

In such places as Peiping the first business of the police every morning for years has been to pick up the corpses of those who starved in the streets during the night.

Thanks chiefly to a few men who gave us our organization of freedom, America is the easiest place to get by in.

The American Constitution, wrote H. G. Wells, was as new as something coming out of an egg. It gave us new rights to "life, liberty and the pursuit of happiness." It gave us something else which was just as new, but which gets hardly any publicity in the school books.

The Constitution gave an unprecedented new freedom to the American businessman. That was as new as the right to vote. It was a radical departure from business practice in Europe and it is different from business practice in most of the world today.

Since Rome crushed the businessman at Carthage, he had known no such freedom. Rome established the politico as the boss of man; and Rome made it the common practice for the politico to live by loot. Rome barred the businessman, as a shifty huckster, from the best clubs. Rome despised the businessman because he sought profits. It barred him from political authority, no matter how rich he might become. Rome established in the minds of men a contempt for the producer. Work was for slaves; and the tradesman was only one notch higher in the social scale.

It was the Roman view that if eggs were rotting at a nickel a dozen in Syracuse when they were worth a dollar a dozen in Rome, then somebody should eat the surplus hens. Nobody but the tricky tradesman would think of moving eggs. The Roman politico never could see—and our political softies cannot see to this day—that the tradesman would thereby make both Rome and Syracuse richer. What the politico could see was that the tradesman would make a profit, which in the Roman mind was close to stealing. The politico could see no profit in the deal for himself. So he was inclined to put a new tax on the tradesman and on the excess hens. So the Roman politico piled control upon control and tax upon tax until the empire collapsed in the glittering poverty of its political dry rot and the agonies of starving slaves.

This contempt for the producer was common also among the Greeks and it is still common in much of the world. When the American revolution freed the businessman to bring forth the greatest egg production known to man, it did not cure the old Roman in us.

Rome and Greece taught men that they must trust the politico to be wise and honest because he pretends to be above profit. Such faith in the politico has seldom been justified. The politico also seeks profit; and he seeks it without producing. That means that he must "control" the marketplace where the money is made. It means that he must bully and hijack the businessman who makes the money.

Business in Europe was subject to the dictates of the non-producing nobles of the royal courts. In England men had to get a "royal license" to do business; they then had to submit to trade associations and price agreements which had the effect of holding up weak producers—and therefore prices—to this day. It was the usual practice for English and other Kings to grant "royal monopolies" to the dukes and barons most favored in court, with freedom of competition emphatically forbidden by law. In Europe they are called "cartels."

The French revolution got rid of one such noble crowd. Then in the name of democracy it brought forth the most pervasive group of official loafers who ever oppressed producers short of communism. From them a farmer was supposed to get official permission in triplicate to cut down a tree or build a hen-house and, of course, wait a year or so to get it. There was another great outburst of liberty and democracy in Latin America. It was liberty of a Roman variety. Here these Latin heirs of Caesar are still exhibiting some of the finest samples of official fungus on business since Cato. It is common practice for the dictator—or other politico in a fake democracy—to invite the businessman to cut him in on the profits, with the alternative that the dictator's brother-in-law would take over the business.

That is the sort of business practice which has often straitjacketed business in many parts of the world.

The businessman is the natural prey of the conquering politico.

All such official regulating and royal grafting on business is sure to bring forth one result. That is to hobble, shackle or ruin business. It was most completely ruined in the Dark Ages when the profit motive itself was damned as sinful.

The businessman never can be expected anywhere to risk his money and his sweat to produce what the politico can take away from him.

The American revolution brought forth an unheard of "freedom of competition." The Constitution imposed drastic restriction on the politico's powers. It gave the businessman protection against official grafters in the courts. He was subject to the laws forbidding such sins as murder and larceny, but in the field of production he had such freedom as had never been known. The world of business became a sort of jungle of free competition.

It was the objective of the businessman to get the money. Many a hijacker and chiseler raided the caravan, from John Jacob Astor to the five percenters. In the general sunlight of the Constitution, however, there has always been some prejudice against larceny and freedom to expose it. The main effort had to be on production. His new freedom gave the businessman an unprecedented freedom, security and incentive to produce.

In nearly all the world the best brains had been going into non-productive politics or religion or war. That was where the power and security were; and that is where they still are in much of the world. In America the best brains turned to production. That is where the power and money have been in America.

In the free competition of this business jungle the Carnegies and Fords could amass millions. All they had to do was to give the world an unheard of production of steel and cars.

In the generation of uproar about the sins of the "robber barons," the "muckrackers" always neglected the most important fact. *That was that the barons had to produce. They might "conquer a continent," but in the process they had to build the most far-flung and efficient railroad system and lead the world in doing it*. So it went, not only in the high places, but also in the thousands of low places throughout this business jungle,—in all of our farms and factories and stores—with other enterprising souls amassing their millions by planting orange trees in Florida wastes. All they had to do to get their millions was to give us more orange juice at lower prices!

In this jungle of free competition the great lions often revealed a shocking lack of morality and social responsibility. They bribed legislators, bought and corrupted newspapers, and worked their employees like Roman slave-drivers. Some of the lions came to believe they could buy anything. They were soon conniving with monopolies and tariffs to escape the rigors of the freedom in which they had grown.

His new freedom permitted the businessman at times to perpetrate atrocities. Such atrocities never were as bad as those political Neros perpetrated in other lands. There was always that sunlight of the Constitution in which poisons produced their own antidotes. It gave the victims their unchallenged freedom to protest. They have protested. One result is that the businessman finds himself in his present precarious situation.

The American Constitution has not given us the

Utopia of the philosopher's dreams. It has given us something. It has given American babies more milk than babies ever had before in the history of the world.

3

Utopias Must Face the Facts

The American Constitution
was largely the work of businessmen. It reveals
the twenty centuries of Graeco-Roman psychosis in
us that we are still ashamed of that fact. We teach
that our heroes were politicos.

Our teachers may tell the children about all those
other political freedoms which other democracies
have imitated—the freedoms of press, religion and
speech—but they avoid talking about that peculiarly American freedom which gives us most of
the automobiles in the world. They are skittish
about those restrictions on the politico which gave
a great new freedom to the businessman. They do
not emphasize this American variety of freedom
for the producer to produce and profit as a matter
of right, which has made America so different from
those democracies where the politico's first concern

has been to control the marketplace. So it is that many children may not even hear about it until their last years in college. Then they may hear we might lose it.

Franklin and Jefferson were capitalists before they were intellectually daring radicals. They were successful businessmen before they were revolutionary dreamers. Washington was the richest man in the colonies before his decision not to be king revealed the realistic political philosopher. They were three of the ablest businessmen who ever entered politics.

In one of his early books, *An Economic Interpretation of the Constitution of the United States,* Charles Beard showed that it was the businessmen of the colonies who were the most influential in obtaining acceptance for that revolutionary document. He showed that many of them owned depreciated revolutionary bonds. They had risked their money as well as their lives for the revolution.

The book caused a furore. Many of the critics seemed to think it was an outrage to accuse our heroes of being businessmen. There were hints that only a Bolshevik could say such a thing in front of schoolboys.

THE BUSINESSMAN MUST SAVE HIMSELF

It reveals the Roman psychosis in our own American subconscious that such critics can accept the most atrocious larcenies and massacres by the politico as the normal order in human affairs, as it has been for so many centuries. These critics, however, are scandalized that the lowly businessman should try to make a profit, even if he must break all production records to do so. Beard's critics were shocked that the financial backers of the revolution should even try to get their own money back.

Our Constitution gave this great new freedom to the businessman by the device of imposing checks and balances upon political rulers.

It is those restrictions on the politico which make the Constitution the despair of all those in government who would like to take over greater control of business. It is the freedom which the Constitution gives to the businessman which in our times caused many a New Dealer to assail the "nine old men" as "constitutional bigots."

For the businessman with a plan for production, political freedom is a first necessity. That means he can risk his money and sweat in safety from robbers, particularly the official grafters who have straitjacketed business nearly everywhere and always. It means that he will not be harassed by police as long as he runs his business honestly. It means that the politico may not horn in on his profits with exorbitant taxes or "controls" of his markets. That has always been the chief racket of the politico. He rigs the market with "controls" in favor of the businessmen who support him.

This peculiarly American business freedom is the essential freedom which has earned for us most of the wealth in the world. It is this freedom which is the chief issue in the great world war of ideas between Left and Right. America has had more of that freedom than any other country in history. Communist Russia has none of it. It is this specific freedom which is the specific hate of all communists. It is also the specific hate of all those of whatever political complexion who would curb that freedom in America.

In this great new freedom, the American producer was given an unheard of security and incentive to produce. In this freedom of producer and consumer, the American businessman was given unheard of rewards for finding the markets which made production worth while. In that freedom he could risk his sweat and money to bring forth the economic grandeur of the United States.

The jungle of free competition, however, was never an anarchy. It was subject to the same laws as the rest of us; and in addition it had some laws of its own. One of them was as severe as any ever devised by any politico, with penalty more dreadful and certain. *This law ordained that if a man invest his money foolishly, then he must lose that money.* That is the most important law in the economic life of man.

What to do with the surplus from his sweat always must be the decision which demands from man the ultimate in wisdom, prudence and enterprise. If the investor makes a mistake, then the sweat is wasted, the surplus is lost; grass grows in the streets, and babies may cry for milk in vain. If the new shoe factory is profitable, then the whole town may share in the prosperity.

In the cruelly free competition of our business jungle, America's decisions on where to invest its surplus have been made by experts. They always had to prove their expertness in the simplest but most exacting of tests. *That was in earning and saving some surplus to invest.*

They were experts who knew their own business well enough to risk their own money in it; or they knew their business well enough to prove to bankers and others that the surplus in their custody would be safe. That means that the economic strength of the United States has grown from the independent and dynamic intelligence of any and all investors —many thousands of them, large and small,—who had to prove their economic wisdom first by getting the surplus to invest and then again by investing it productively.

The penalty for making a silly investment is financial death for the businessman. The penalty for making a silly investment by his old adversary, the politico, is loss by all the rest of us.

This matter of investing the surplus from man's sweat presents the most important difference between the original American system and any or all systems of government control of business. It has been side-stepped by all left-wingers. It is evaded by those professors who write about capitalism as disintegrating. What they like to talk about is who gets the dividends. They evade the hard part. *That is, producing the dividends*.

Where such intellectuals win political control,

the system of investing the surplus is different. In communist lands the final decision on how to invest such surplus is made by a politburo. The economic wisdom of such politicians, however, has not been proved in the jungle of business competition. Their business judgment has not been tested by the exacting problems of how to produce better goods at lower prices. Their genius is not in production. They are not producers at all.

On the contrary, politicians are tempted to be cynical and unscrupulous parasites. The whole nature of the politician's business requires a different sort of talent. They must prove their genius in that special and different business of conniving, shouting or toadying their way into office. In the communist lands, such non-productive geniuses are entrusted with the investment of whatever surplus their slaves may produce. Communism gives them totalitarian authority over all the complex machinery of production and all its fruits. If they invest the surplus foolishly, they do not lose it personally. For that heinous and disastrous offense of silly investment which in capitalism is always punished with financial death, the communist politico may suffer no personal penalty at all.

It is the communist dream that such politicians always will be honest and skillful investors of the surplus from their slaves' sweat because they may have read Marx. It is their fond hope that the non-productive politico may know more about the infinitely difficult problems of production than producers.

It is the belief of the starry-eyed that such economic childishness is something new. It was old when the communist slaves of Egypt were building the pyramids. It always has brought forth general poverty. It never could bring forth anything else.

This essential defect in communist procedure is vital. It may be sufficient in itself to assure the eventual doom of the police state. It may not. The politico never can be expected to be an expert in production, but the communist politicos have shown great genius in wielding police clubs and propaganda. With police clubs and propaganda they may conquer us.

What to do with the surplus from his sweat remains a most important and permanent problem in the life of man. It is the communist faith that men may best trust the politico with that decision. The businessmen who gave us our Constitution entrusted that decision to the owners of the property which was being risked. It gave them a maximum of freedom, power and responsibility. That system is relatively new. It has brought forth the greatest production known to man. But it can be expected to fall when too many owners fail at their job.

4

The Social Planners

If the businessman is to win any sympathy from the jury he had better admit the truth. The truth is that the businessman had been running things and 1932 showed he had made some disastrous mistakes.

It is one of the weaknesses of capitalism that the owners of the money are so chary about investing their surplus into circulation when "business is bad." That means depressions are prolonged. If the businessman expects to win acquittal, he had better have answers ready for the next time that employment, profits and the stock market crash.

Whenever private capitalists fail at their job, then the government becomes the obvious agency to correct the failure. The obvious thing for the government to do is to "prime the pump" by using its credit for investment; and some of the power projects appear to have been successful investments. It seems possible that there is a large field where state capitalism might do a better job than private investors. Whether there is or not, the public will demand that the government do the job whenever the owners of the money ignore the crying of babies.

This government spending has resulted in the government's using its credit to encourage a lot of buying on easy payments. The complete story of such investment spending cannot be told until the tax collector comes around asking for his billions.

To keep the record straight, it must never be forgotten that every dollar of the billions poured out by the politicos represented the surplus from some American's sweat. Every dollar ever spent by any legislator or social planner in Washington or elsewhere always must come from the sweat of some citizen. There is no other place for it to come from.

Stupid waste could not be tolerated in the jungle of American business competition. It liquidated inefficiency by bankruptcy and penalized the smallest error in judgment. The jungle sent to Skid Row the silly investor who thought coke should be produced in Florida. The jungle gave its rich rewards to those enterprising souls who could find and evaluate a

Mesabi iron mountain and then risk their own money to give us the mountain in the form of hammers, harvesting machines and automobiles.

Private investment always must be in the public interest, or the public will send the investor to Skid Row. It must be the eternal objective of the businessman to meet the customers' demands. If he fails, they will doom him to bankruptcy even for the slight error of locating his store on the wrong side of the street.

The politico is not necessarily a worse character than the businessman. Our own history is full of the names of brave and honest La Follettes risking their careers to save us from the extortions of others.

Any American politician who has a talent for business has a huge job always confronting him. That is to keep businessmen honest. Our Constitution gave businessmen their freedom; they have been conniving at ways to escape the rigors of that freedom ever since. Their most common racket is the monopoly or "price agreement"—to restrict free competition and gouge the rest of us. Until the politico achieves more success at preventing such frauds by businessmen, we can be skeptical about any and all plans for him to take over the business.

5

Why Utopias Fail

Since Plato wrote
his *The Republic*, brave thinkers have been painting
bright word pictures of those imaginary societies in
which men could escape the cruelties and injustices
of our wicked world. In the greatest of these dreams,
Sir Thomas More gave them their name, *Utopia*.
A history of these Utopias is a record of the brightest
dreams of man. It is also a record of his intellectual
growth.

He has often tried to put these dreams into practice. There have been hundreds of Oneida colonies
where men sought to create the ideal society of their
dreams. There are always men trying to escape from
bitter realities. In the dark ages they fled to monas-
teries, later they fled Europe to America, and in
America they fled to the frontiers, always with hope
of reaching Utopia. One of the things they seek to

escape is the lash of the businessman trying to make profits. To do that, he must get the work done. In the dreams of man the businessman nearly always appears in the role of villain.

Most of these Utopias quickly withered. The record of failure has been so constant that the word itself has come to connote to most men "dreams that fail." The Utopians nearly all made the same mistake. They barred the businessman and his profits. They entrusted the management of their affairs to much nicer fellows whom they elected to office. To such fellows, getting the work done was always a secondary consideration. What they needed first was votes.

Such idealists assumed that most men are fine fellows. Their Utopias failed when they could not supply enough milk for the babies.

Among all these dreams of men for a better world, there has been one which has had considerable success. That was the dream which brought forth the American revolution and the Constitution of the United States. This was the work of tough and able realists. To avoid being hanged by the British, they had to be. It was chiefly the work of business philosophers with a realistic flair for the kind of planning which all organized effort requires.

The success of this American dream has been largely the success of the planful businessman. He it was who linked Pennsylvania coal to Minnesota iron to give us most of the steel in the world. He it was who flung railroads across the continent while men ruled by politicos in so many other lands continue today to ride on the backs of asses. He it was who made the oil fields flow while richer fields in Mexico and Iran are political grease spots. He it was who loaded fast freight trains with California lettuce when Lower California remained a desert. He it was whose genius for production gave American soldiers the most guns, the thickest steaks and the sturdiest vehicles to win world wars. He it was who has so organized our production that even his shaky dollar may overshadow the earth.

The businessman and investor have made our country rich; and from these riches most other blessings have flowed. From the wealth of the businessman's creation all other phases of life could find nourishment—the biggest libraries, hospitals and schools. His genius for production permitted him to pay the highest wages for the shortest hours. He has given us such freedom from want that we are said to waste more food than we eat. In that abundance even the failure in Skid Row may find in his flophouse a comfort and freedom of which most of the citizens in the world may only dream.

For these achievements, the businessman has received little glory. According to the left-wingers, it was the "workers" who did that. They have not explained why such "workers" never created such wealth anywhere else in the uncounted ages of work. They assert it was the inventor who brought forth the industrial revolution. They always neglect to mention that it was the businessman who had the courage to finance the invention and put it to work. When the first steam engine was invented at Alexandria University two thousand years ago, it was used only to astound the public by secretly opening church doors. Then for eighteen centuries it rusted while the intelligentsia damned the profit motive as sinful. It was finally put to work by English businessmen after they succeeded in cutting a royal politico's head off.

6

The Intellectuals

One of the glittering results of the American Revolution has been the American millionaire.

His money gave him power. With it he could buy political power. It had been the age-long practice in other lands for the politico to harass and despoil the businessman. In America the businessman soon learned to corrupt and bully the politico. Nobody was easier to bribe than the political boss.

In the glory of the plutocracy the politico was reduced to the role of the businessman's stooge. So were many other nonproducers. They included some of the most illustrious newspaper and magazine editors, professors, and holy men. They got on Mammon's payroll; or they found themselves on the outside looking in. They became "tools" of the "interests."

All such intellectuals have twenty centuries of Greek, Roman and European tradition to tell them that the producer is an inferior fellow. If they concede that it is the wisdom of the American businessman that has made America so productive and rich that most of the world appears a slum in comparison, then they must admit that their own wisdom is trivial or phony or both.

It has been easier to believe that the millionaire was a tricky swindler or an exploiter of labor. So many of them were.

The millionaire has often been an ignorant fellow outside of his business, stupid and blind to the social and political responsibilities in the power of his money. Like so many Roman big shots of old, the successful businessmen were soon building the grandest palaces of all times. The Greek concept of "elegance without extravagance" was foreign to many American millionaires and their families. They revealed, however, the complex of inferiority by scrambling to curtsy to Europe's royalty and by buying titles. The tabloid editors gloated over their extravagances.

To all onlookers who considered themselves superior to the producer, the spectacle could be

33

nothing less than abhorrent. The café philosophers of Europe snickered about the chase for the dollars in the bath tub civilization. The Southern planters once revolted against the businessman's iniquities. A century of lookers-on who had trouble getting on the payroll never ceased to yap at his heels. Our *illuminati* of the Left Bank cawed at the Rotonde for 29 days a month about the futilities of Babbitt, then crossed the river to the American Express Company on the 30th to get their checks from Babbitt. Such intellects refused to concede intellectual genius in getting a million dollars. The philosophers told them it could not be done honestly.

Triumphant in his jungle, the American millionaire was sometimes as contemptuous as any jungle lion of lesser breeds. He felt that he could ignore such gabblers. He crushed them at the polls with slush funds. He elected a long line of presidents, with the mayors of the palace running things from New York.

His views on human questions depended chiefly on whether business was good. Deriving his wisdom from the financial page, he might have voted for Harding or Coolidge or Judas Iscariot if business was good. In his days of glory the businessman exhorted Americans to buy on easy payments and spend all they could earn or borrow. So the question about whether business was good depended chiefly on how he got on with bankers, tax collectors and customers. About once in each generation, the money lenders asked for their money; or they got it by the simple expedient of selling their creditor's securities. This caused the "reaction" about which Sir Isaac Newton talked in 1687. The combined actions of the businessmen and the bankers resulted in the Business Cycle. 829008

Triumphant in the power of his money, the businessman often has been too short-sighted to know that his Constitution did not give him political power. It merely gave him the freedom to win power if he could earn the votes. He often preferred to buy the votes. It seemed cheaper and quicker.

Arrogantly he drifted into 1929 and then helplessly he groped through the long night. When he could not buy or borrow his way out, he was lost. The problems of depression "glut" confused him. In 1932 the businessman in his social and political responsibilities had failed. His ideological bankruptcy was plain to all in the general poverty and crashing of banks. The businessman had wrecked his own Utopia. He could not stop the baby's crying.

With the businessman's failure, the politico seized power.

7

The Big Unchallenged Lie

The businessman is the goose who laid America's golden eggs. He is the most successful producer in history, but his golden eggs have not helped him much in his public relations. The public knows that what he is after is golden eggs for himself. He is the driver who makes us work for our share of the eggs. He is the economic boss who wields the influence to get the work done.

His jungle of free competition is a cruel place. His lash can be felt in the tempo of big city crowds hurrying back from their lunches. He is the benefactor who hires us at the highest wages on earth; but he is also the executioner who fires us. Any defense of him must always rest on the bitterest facts of life. With his lash on our backs, those facts may seem too cruel for most of us to face.

In the ideological war between Left and Right,

there is a grotesque intellectual curiosity. The most important and obvious truth about the whole business is never publicly stated. Capitalists and communists alike evade it. It is obvious enough to anybody who ever tried to get anything done, but plain statement of it is avoided.

We never are going to get as much as we might in any kind of society, capitalist or communist, *for the simple but inescapable reason that many of us are of little value as voluntary producing workers.*

Apparently this obvious truth is considered too painful for most of us to face. The capitalist does not dare to print it in his own newspaper. Senators would consider it bad politics. So any rational defense of the businessman has to be hamstrung by this avoidance of the truth.

The big unchallenged lie is that we are all competent, noble, industrious, and deserving.

The bitter truth is that most of us in the present economic set-up are physically or mentally unfit to give all the voluntary help we might toward keeping our country prosperous.

We have only to look around to see that most of us do not like to work. We will do it only when economic necessity makes us do it.

THE BUSINESSMAN MUST SAVE HIMSELF

Such is the bitter truth which the businessman must face every day that he goes to his desk. It is his business to get the work done. It is his painful duty to tell so many of us that we are not good enough competently to help him do it.

But truth is the only solid foundation for any rational order in human affairs; and any attempt to base society upon a lie invites disaster. The communists in power had to face the fact. So must every politico of whatever promise when the hopeful voters trust him with the responsibilities of production, from the first old man of the first tribe to Stalin, and from Caesar to Perón. Wherever men must eat, somebody must produce. Demanding production, the communists quickly discovered that many citizens were not competent producers.

To get work done without incentive, there could be only one recourse. That was to use police clubs. From police clubs the road is always straight and certain to plots, purges, tortures, planned starvation and "confessions."

The communist production records did not justify their hopes. After years of police clubbing the communists still give their production figures in percentages. Of course they soon revived competition among workers to make them work harder, but they could not revive it on the executive levels where it is most important. They could not inspire creative genius with police clubs or convict labor camps. Such men must have hard-boiled intellectual daring. Their success always must be based on experiment. In Russia they could expect to be liquidated if the experiment failed. The creative genius by which such men have raised us from the primeval swamp never can grow in the shadow of the policeman.

The American revolution invited such creatively daring souls to produce. That was how they could win wealth and power. The Russian revolution invited the best brains into party politics; there they could get limousines. The result was certain and inevitable. That is, hopeless poverty for the majority.

Communists still point to Skid Row as proof of capitalist sin. They claim that is where America sends many of its citizens who are not much good as workers. The Russians substituted for Skid Row the most gigantic and cruel hells known in their slave labor camps.

8

The Weak Links

The Spartans seized them young and put them on the mountain top to die. The Romans fed them to the lions. The Russians liquidate them in slave labor camps. In Christian lands there always has been an honest attempt to be more merciful.

What to do about the fellow who is no good, or not eager for voluntary work, always must be one of the first problems in any kind of society, beginning in the family itself.

The fellow who chops off the roots when he hoes the corn, who is too lazy to get to work on time, who hunts the gas leak with matches, and trumps his partner's aces,—these are perennially with us. There is the plumber who joins pipes so they will leak, the dentist who pulls the wrong teeth, and the bus driver who races trains to crossings. His intentions are good, but he is weak.

Then there is the smarty who passes the phony check, the policeman who takes bribes, the contractor who adulterates the cement, the doctor who lets his poor patients die, and the columnist who tells half the truth and leaves a big lie to the imagination. Those surely are fellows who are not good enough. They are the weak links in the mesh of our complex society which break when we must depend upon them.

As everybody knows, the object of such people in life is to get by. At that they often develop a certain kind of skill, so that public and private bureaucracies become infested with them. For the businessman who must produce to profit, they are the eternal headache.

It is obvious that when there are too many of these weak links in any business, the business must fail. When there are enough of these weak links in the interdependent mesh of our society, then it is the society itself which must sag in decay and finally break down. When there are enough of them in Washington, then no Constitution may save us from the collapse which all decayed peoples have suffered.

It is relatively simple to defend ourselves against criminals; we can call the police. It is difficult to defend ourselves against the silly telephone girl who gives us the wrong number and the blundering nitwit who loses the precious papers in the wrong file. Even the mighty king who challenged armies could not defend himself against the fatuous bungler who forgot the nail that might have saved the kingdom. Such are the weak links who cause so much of the trouble in the world.

In the days of unbridled capitalism, there was a procedure for dealing with this weak link which was simple and salutary. That was to fire him. He might have another chance to wake up and produce if he could get another job, but nobody else could be expected to feed him. If he did not produce, he could die in Skid Row, along with his wife and babies.

That was a heartless procedure, as cruel as the jungle which in fact the world of business once was. It caused widespread anguish and wailing among the weak links. It caused the slums of Oliver Twist and Jean Valjean to be oceans of misery. Their wails were heard in an era of protest. This protest fermented from Dickens and Hugo to Marx, exploded after a generation of Upton Sinclairs in Lenin, and boiled over everywhere in the long depression. It has produced the great social-political uproar of our times and divided the whole world into two camps.

This was a protest which appealed to the most high-minded of men. It does yet. The reason is not difficult to find. It is that *among the weakest links are stupid capitalists and producers.* It has been easy for any leftist to show that these have included the most vicious and stupid pirates, slave traders, drivers, and an infinite variety of other thieves and scoundrels—and perhaps nearly all of their heirs. It was easy to show that the capitalist often robbed the inventor, hogged the profits of his business, and gave his employees a tiny fraction of their output for their work. Capitalists won control of this world with the power of their brains, industry and money. The quality of their rule has been shown by recurrent wars and depressions, climaxed by the bloodiest of world wars and the longest depression.

Against such crimes of rich fellows, and especially those who inherited their wealth, the world has revolted. It always has been a chief weakness of capitalism that it gives power to whoever has money; and it always is so easy to show that many of the rich fellows are irresponsible. The revolt has been marked by a confusion about what capitalism really is. It has no manifesto or Constitution. The capitalists themselves are a most diversified assortment of good and bad men of all nationalities. If they have any common ideology, it is that of rich fellows trying to hang on to their money. They seek to protect anybody who can show legal title to money.

The defense of capitalism would be easier if men could assume that most of those who have money deserve it. It is impossible to conduct a census to determine whether the owners of the money deserve it or not. So the drive against the abuses in capitalism has been a drive for reform in the rules whereby men can get and keep money. The last two centuries have seen revolutions in the rules. Some of the most potent reformers were capitalists. The chief reformer of British factories was factory owner Robert Owen, with a long list of conscientious heirs among American businessmen. The weaknesses and abuses in the capitalist structure have now become obvious even to the editors of the *Wall Street Journal*.

This protest against capitalist vices, however, soon went beyond any purpose of correcting abuses. Defending the victims of such vices, it soon got itself entangled in the obvious absurdity that all such victims are good. Driving for popular support, it was soon asserting the obvious lie that all "underdogs" are noble and deserving victims of capitalists, who are all scoundrels. The goal of these extreme left-wingers was not to correct the abuses of capitalism but to destroy the producers themselves.

The program was so simple that any simpleton could understand it. They would haul down the rich and take their money. And then what? They would take away the infinitely complex machinery of production from the owners and turn it over to the commissars, guaranteeing that they would be fine, honest, competent producers.

Such is the red program. The crimes and stupidities of capitalists have been so great that about one-third of the world has gone communist. It has been the most drastic social purge known. If called upon to justify it, the reds might show that many of the victims deserved what they got. They can easily show that many of the rich fellows in Poland or Bulgaria were stupid or anti-social parasites, as most of them may be in Honduras and Spain now. In the abounding poverty and corruption of those countries the reds could show the cynical irresponsibility of the wealthy land owners. What the communists cannot show is improvement in the fate of their own followers. They still offer promises. They still shout "you have nothing to lose but your chains." Yet they have given to their dupes the heaviest chains in the world.

This Russian debacle may have shattered the faith in the Kremlin of many of our leftists, but it has not shattered their faith in the big lie at the bottom of the revolution.

Unlike the Russians, they have not yet discovered that many of the citizens are not much good as workers or creators. The philosophy of such softies is still based on the most absurd lie of our times—the lie that the drones, incompetents, thieves and assorted weak links are all equally noble and deserving.

In Britain the government undertook to give security from the cradle to the grave. They evaded the plain fact that the only way any government can feed the loafers must be at the expense of every honest producer who must produce the food.

In the complexities of modern living, this truth, so obvious to the first tribe thousands of years ago, may be temporarily obscured. A strong labor union may compel the boss to feed many incompetents until he nearly goes broke—and that may foolishly be interpreted as a "social gain" for "labor." The shyster politico may feed many boondogglers with government funds, thus buying their votes until the government nears bankruptcy. Any realist knows that such proceedings must be temporary. The process amounts to feeding the unfit at the expense of the fit, upholding drones at the expense of producers, glorifying the dishonest at the expense of the honest, promoting weakness at the expense of strength. That process cannot be permanent. The reason is simple. It is an outright violation of the first and fundamental law of an implacable Deity who has ordained that the fit shall survive. When the softies elect to challenge that law, they may profess to believe that man is such a superior mammal that he may get away with it. But they can offer no evidence, only hope. All the evidence is that any power that attempts to uphold weakness at the expense of strength shall decay and die.

What ought to be done about the weak link remains the question to intimidate philosophers. The lookers-on must find the question unpalatable. The bitterest duty of the doctor is to tell the man with cancer that he will probably die; what the sufferer wants is hope. In the fields of philosophy or politics or literature, evasion is so much easier. It is so easy to evade the bitter truth by asserting that all the unfortunates in the world are so because of what capitalism has made them. There is just enough truth in that to make plausible the most gigantic lie of our times. So the softies may evade the truth and give us hope. The hope they offer is in changing the system. So until that system is changed, what to do about the weak link is off the subject for them. They prefer to believe that all of us would be fine fellows if the capitalists would give us a chance.

In the meantime the businessman would like to fire the weak link and forget him. He cannot forget him as long as he votes. He cannot even fire a man who is a member of the right labor union.

Perhaps the best answer already has been given by the philosophers who wrote our Constitution. One could imagine the cold eyes of George Washington surveying the question and leaving the answer unspoken but implicit in that freedom.

The Constitution permits even to the weakest link his vote.

It gives him his eternal freedom to wake up and

produce if he can get another job, with a better chance of finding that job than he could ever have in any denial of that freedom.

In the abundance which producers could create in that freedom, it gives even the failure in his flophouse on Skid Row a comfort and independence of which weak links in unhappier lands cannot even dream, with the eternal freedom to get out and produce.

It could give even to the convict in an American prison, at the depth of our longest depression, a higher standard of material comfort than the ordinary citizen has ever known in any one of history's hundreds of police states.

As long as that freedom lasts in America, the weak link will eat, drink and vote. He will often vote against the businessman. It was the businessman who fired him.

9

Debt and Depressions

In the first chapter of her monumental *History of the Business Man* Miriam Beard concluded ". . . the businessman has never recovered from the seal of inferiority which was stamped upon him during the Roman conquests. . . . It is entirely within the bounds of possibility that the Battle of Zama ended for all time his chance to rule the earth. . . ."

At times since that historic date the businessman has emerged from his tomb in brief resurrections. He has seldom lasted very long. The merchants of Venice and Florence regained considerable freedom from the eternal enemy, the politico. They soon lost it to the cannons which they sold to royal politicos. So did the Dutch and German burghers. In England the businessmen beheaded a king and then expanded their business until the sun never set upon it, only to be "nationalized" in the world conflict now going on.

There have been numerous instances in which the wisest of politicos have granted to the businessman great freedom, which is different from the businessman winning power himself. In Germany and Japan he was permitted enough freedom to create great prosperity, subject to the politico's controls. Even in certain Latin American countries, the politico can see that there will not be much swag to steal if the businessman is not permitted some freedom to create it.

The greatest resurgence of the businessman has occurred in the United States. Here a few of the ablest businessmen who ever entered politics established his freedom to produce and profit as a matter of right. They did not give him power. They gave him the freedom to earn or buy it. It now seems possible that the American businessman may have reached a zenith of power in the Coolidge prosperity.

In all of his brief resurrections, the weakness of the businessman has been easy to see. He is nearly always too busy making money to defend himself or to bother about the public health. His business has been to create wealth for himself; when the public or the country gets rich in the process, that is incidental. He never has been greatly concerned, not even in America, with the rules. Generations of American businessmen have been busy concocting swindles against those rules, such as monopolies, tariffs and "price agrements." It is not necessary to visit the high places to see the indifference of the businessman to the freedom which gives him his own power.

The businessman has not trusted the public. There is nothing more incongruous than a supposed robber appealing to the public conscience! Even if he is the most altruistic of public benefactors, he knows the power of his money is the envy of his fellow men. Recently somebody sold the business- man on the idea of hiring public relations counsel, but these press agents have seemed almost impotent in the ideological war.

There is another weakness in the foundation of capitalism which is so basic that it was obvious to Hammurabi and Moses. That is the mathematical impossibility of paying interest indefinitely on bor- rowed money. It is simple arithmetic that a fortune like King Farouk's at six percent could double in value every twelve years, so that a relatively paltry pile of one hundred million dollars could become nearly thirteen billion dollars for the king's grandchildren to spend. It could snowball into a ball of gold bigger than the earth if it were possible for men to pay the six percent.

What is more important is that men cannot pay six percent for very long on the deluges of gilt and green and purple "securities" which capitalists issue in every boom. The fathers of Christian, Jew and Moslem faiths knew that men could not produce fast enough to pay the interest, so they made "usury" a crime and condemned the money lender to hell, with the Roman fathers being forbidden even to accept such gifts to the Community Chest. It was not until 1830 that Pope Pius VIII told confessors to stop worrying bankers about their business. That date might be taken to indicate the approximate age of modern capitalism.

What made the money lender respectable was the machine and cheap power. With the machine men could produce fast enough to pay the six percent. With it men could even get rich on borrowed money. That was something new. So the money lender became a banker; and as such was welcomed to church and maybe to heaven.

His job now became most important. It was deciding where to invest the surplus from man's sweat. He can claim that it was our blessed savings, with his wisdom, which financed man's greatest expansion of wealth. His biggest and oldest problem remains. That is what to do about that snowballing gold.

"From shirt sleeves to shirt sleeves in three generations" was the happy lie echoed by silly editorial writers. That is the sort of fraud which cannot save the bankers from the modern barbarians. The lawmakers knew better. It may be a sign of hope that they could enact income and estate taxes with which the politico could hack off big chunks from the balls of gold so that idle parasites could not clip coupons forever. That has happened in a few countries. Capitalists have devised "trusts" and "foundations" and "residence in the Bahamas" to avoid the tax collector, apparently in the hope that the balls of gold could continue snowballing.

It remains thus far impossible even for the machine to produce fast enough to meet the promises in those glittering "securities." So it becomes necessary, at intervals, to purge men of their mountains of debt. That is what happens in "depressions." It is in those depressions that the "weak debtors" go bankrupt, heaps of brightly gilded paper go into the ash can, and man's incubus of debt is reduced.

About these depressions the professors of economics have written volumes which reveal that their causes are obscure. What is certain is that they have been occurring once each generation ever since the usurer became a banker, about as regularly as eclipses, so they appear to be a sort of economic necessity in this capitalistic structure. Whatever it is that causes them, it is certain that bankers ask for their money and the sheriff conducts a financial massacre of the borrowers, with incredible bargains for anybody with cash at the sheriff's sales. When the great storm is over, the real wealth is in "strong hands," bankers once more begin lending money to "men of character," and another business cycle begins. Men have been relieved of much of their debt. Many of them also have been relieved of their homes.

After 1912, many hopeful souls thought that the new Federal Reserve system was going to avert depressions forevermore, but the first purge under this new banking system was the longest and worst. The only explanation available was that the politicos in charge of the scheme must have been capitalist stooges. Once more men had been deceived.

It is so easy to see that the inflation of men's paper promises means joyous boom days and deflation of them means depression woe. The solution seems so simple,—just print more dollars! The depression doctors have stuffed the libraries with variations of that theme. What they all overlook is that printing more paper would not rid us of the ever-tightening coils of the six percent interest. We cannot pay six percent on those boom-day promises for long. There are too many of them. We cannot even pay six percent permanently on any paper, for the same reason that it is not possible to transform the earth into gold. It could not rid us of excess paper to print more paper. The new paper would feed the strangler fig as much as it would the strangling oak. It would give temporary relief in paying the six percent and then the tentacles of the monster would still be there to squeeze more tightly than ever.

Conceivably some politico might be shyster enough to print enough paper to buy all other paper on all stock exchanges to end the value of all paper, beginning with government bonds. But any action short of such a paper revolution leaves the six percent monster intact and always growing. Until such a paper revolution occurs, surgery must be necessary to cut off some of the overpowering tentacles. That surgery is supplied in depressions by the sheriff. He rids us of debts with a financial massacre of the debtors.

The term "six percent" as used here is a symbol. The billions owing on installment purchases call for more than six percent. Most bonds pay less. The lower the interest rate, the longer it requires the snowball to roll to the end of the "prosperity" cycle.

In the regions around Broad and Wall Streets, sophisticated realists may feel that such periodical purging is necessary to save their own six percent. Since there is that indefinite but certain limit to how much the debtors can pay, it must seem that the financial jungle at times must be swept clean of all those weaker vines reaching down for their six percent. To such realists, an occasional hurricane must seem necessary to sweep the jungle clean.

Those depressions are too painful for the rest of

us. Too many good men rot in bread lines, too many go communist, and too many babies all over the world cry for milk which their parents have not the means to buy.

10

The National Conspiracy

If the businessman ever takes the stand in his own defense, the prosecutor will have many questions to ask about depressions. He will have other questions to ask about the businessman's practice of making articles scarce in order to make more money out of them.

The American businessman can truthfully shout that he has broken all the production records in the world. The prosecutor can truthfully shout back that he has been breaking records in also conniving to control prices.

Disgraced by 1932, businessmen wasted much time "hating Roosevelt." They assailed the idiocy of plowing up cotton and massacring female pigs. They became bulbous with rage about bricklayers conspiring to lay fewer bricks.

Such hypocrisy will be incredible for the jury

to behold. It was the businessman himself who taught us to make articles scarcer to get higher prices. He has been doing it for years and bribing the politico to help him do it. He has been the chief conspirator in a nation-wide conspiracy.

Wrote the Scotch economist Adam Smith in 1776: "People of the same trade hardly ever meet together, even for merriment or diversion, but the conversation ends with a conspiracy against the public or with some contrivance to raise prices." More than a century later Charles M. Schwab was saying "not only in steel but in everything else there are similar agreements known as joint agreements to maintain prices. They have existed in all lines of business as long as I can remember."

The system is known to everybody. The producers get together and agree to produce less so they can jack up prices at the public expense. Of course there is bawling to Washington, but the politico is an undependable reed. All the anti-trust uproars in Washington have failed to make much change in the prices of nickel or sulphur, glass or shoe machinery, sleeping cars or bananas. By "stabilizing" their production, such businessmen make bigger immediate profits.

Of course, they can argue that there is no need for more production. "Glut" is the word for it. They have been arguing against "glut" ever since the law of supply and demand gave them their first beating. They have been trying to cheat the law of supply and demand ever since. When they succeed, the victims of their extortions try to do the same thing in self defense. When the price of harvesting machines is "stabilized," the farmers must shout for stabilized wheat. So the bricklayers lay fewer bricks, the farmers vote for the politico who will dye potatoes blue, and so it goes. Finally, the whole country is temporarily engaged in the national conspiracy against abundance to make each other poorer, even to the point where doctors must conspire to make medical service scarcer at the expense of lives.

In his eternal conniving to escape free competition and make commodities scarcer, the businessman has found that the tightest monopolies or "agreements" may not be sufficient. He also requires a tariff. It will do no good to line up all the producers for a high price if the only result is to hand over the market to some wicked foreigner. So he must urge his government to enact a tariff. Tariffs are not a direct factor in causing business depressions although they handicap world business as a whole and we all would probably be richer without them. This tariff problem is primarily a moral problem, as are the liquor problem, the immigration problem, the labor-leader problem, the monopoly problem, the armament problem and the tax problem.

Whatever the magnitude of any of these or other problems, our nation could suffer depression or enjoy prosperity. The major business cycle which gives us these periods of prosperity, decline, depression and improvement seems to be based primarily on debt,—or to speak more exactly, upon the abnormal accelerating or retarding of expansion due to the expanding or reducing of debt. These major cycles average about eighteen years—more or less equal to a generation—and apply especially to employment conditions and the like. Each major cycle is approximately divided into three minor cycles of about six years. The minor cycles are of great importance to bankers, businessmen and investors.

As classic illustrations of how our excess of debt has caused business to collapse in the past, we can refer to: (1) The Railroad Panic of the 1870's caused by the over-expansion of railroad debt; (2) The Western Mortgage Panic of the 1890's caused by the scramble for farm and other mortgages which promised more than six percent interest; (3) The Industrial Panic starting in 1907 because of an excess of debt issued in connection with the formulation of "trusts", consolidations, etc.; (4) The Bankers' Panic of the 1930's allied with the over-expansion of public utility debt promoters.

Our Constitution has given us freedom to make such mistakes. It has given us also freedom to correct the mistakes. All of these great depressions of the past taught lessons. They brought forth legislation aimed to prevent such errors ever happening again. They have not yet taught us not to borrow more than we can pay.

The Panic of the 1950's–60's probably will be called the great Consumers' Panic, resulting from a combination of bullish advertising, installment purchases, undeserved salaries, wages and profits; general extravagance, waste and inefficiency of the individual.

Then once more the marching interest rates will overtake the capacity of men to produce to pay. Once more the creditor will call on men for his money. Once more the outraged citizens will shout that they cannot find work, that the businessman has failed, that the politico must take over because the businessman has proved a scoundrel.

So once more all men must suffer because the businessman in his American freedom has failed to confront his own problems with the morality and responsibility which the power of his money demands. Once more the citizens may well have to call on the non-productive politico for the leadership which business leaders have failed to exercise.

In this swiftly passing present, the citizens have given the business leaders of America another chance. If their wisdom is limited to getting onto the short side before the crash, they must not be surprised if the next depression may be their last.

His money gives the businessman power. It is the history of the businessman that he always has lost that power because he did not exercise it with the responsibility which men have the right to demand. He always has been too busy making more money.

Of all such moral problems confronting the business leader in these decisive days, the anomaly which must cause him the most soul-searching must be his own tariff. That political control of the market is his own creation. For a century he has been asserting that it is the basis of American prosperity. It is the tariff which has permitted many a factory to keep busy, which has allowed many an industry to live and grow. It is also the tariff which has permitted many a business racketeer to make a "price agreement" to keep up prices at the public expense. It is now the tariff which forbids Europeans to produce goods which Americans would like to buy. It is the American tariff which has set the style for similar tariffs to straitjacket business and production in all the world. It is the American tariff which compels the American businessman to pay billions in taxes from his profits to save the world from Communism in the business wreckage and poverty for which restrictions on trade are partly responsible. Such tariffs are the chief obstruction to normal world trade—and, therefore, production.

Since the days of the "full dinner pail," it has been the argument that tariffs are necessary to protect American industry from the competition of cheap foreign labor. The competent businessman does not need a professor of economics to tell him that every dollar which Americans pay for anything

THE BUSINESSMAN MUST SAVE HIMSELF

they buy elsewhere must be spent for American goods in return. He could expect the greatest boom in American production history as markets of all the world were compelled—by economic necessity—to open to all those products which Americans make best and cheapest. These include wheat and cotton, automobiles and adding machines, a whole catalog of the products of American farms and factories.

It is easy to imagine the threat of Communism vanishing in an unheard of prosperity in the entire free world as producers actually were set free to produce and markets were open to the most competent producers, workers and consumers. We could expect a renaissance of Europe if the creative and productive genius of that continent were set free to produce instead of cadging American relief. We could expect a great American boom *based on honest production*, not on those gilded promises to pay. Other writers may well expand on the possibilities of that unheard of prosperity that can occur when the producers at last are freed both from abnormal debt and from the political shackles on business and labor. May some of the intelligentsia get their dreams to working on how to utilize the genius of the businessman in such a new business freedom instead of condemning him to the controls of the politico which always fail.

Such a dream may be too much for some of our manufacturers. It would be painful to those businessmen who are now honestly asking for a tariff to prevent unemployment in their communities. Reducing tariffs could be costly to producers and wage workers who cannot produce well enough to stand free competition.

There are businessmen to whom moral reforms might seem to threaten bankruptcy. Simple justice may require that such reforms be gradual. It seems likely, however, that it is easier to exaggerate that threat. Perhaps any businessman or wage earner who cannot stand competition on his present line could easily convert for other demands. Such conversion is going on all the time. The end of war compels all industry to reconvert for peace. There must have been many threatened industries in every state when the Constitution opened to all the world's largest free market. The threat becomes less ominous with the promise of greater general prosperity.

Whatever the threat to the "hard headed" businessman such moral reforms may entail, it can hardly be greater than that other threat in his trial for his life. It cannot benefit him to keep his factory operating today if it costs him his home tomorrow. It cannot benefit him to make profits if they are to vanish largely through inflation and taxes. His profits must be questionable when he must pour out billions to save the world from communism in the business wreckage which his moral carelessness helps to create.

He cannot hope for the politico to save him from his own sins. If he has the wisdom of those businessmen who gave him his Constitution he will know that he must save himself;—and that he must strip for action in his biggest fight to clean out the mistakes in his own house.

11

Is Another 1932 Depression Necessary?

It is the businessman's technique, whenever the politico turns the public spotlight into some dark corner of the market place, to shout "Communism!"

It is easy to predict that Russian communism is destined to become a failure. It is not difficult to show that our own pinks are silly frauds. What is not so easy is to prove that our own businessmen are wise. Too many of them are governed by hopes and hunches rather than by impartial statistics.

It is not the truth in Russian communism that permits it to advance. Communists have never won an honest national election anywhere. They never deceive a majority of the voters. What permits communism to advance is the corruption and poverty which the people are suffering.

Whenever capitalism becomes too careless, the

reds have only to push it over. It is sufficient that honest men should quit defending it. That has been the history of communism to date. They merely have moved in as the capitalist world failed, piece by piece.

Wherever the red fraud has triumphed, it has been so easy to show that too many capitalists were fools. Most of the rich of Eastern Europe did not deserve the responsibility of their wealth. Their property was of little value to anybody but themselves. If they ever used their power to promote political health or business honesty or a safe milk supply in their countries, their influence was invisible. They were more likely to invest the power from their slaves' sweat in cocottes on the Rue Pigalle.

If there is one lesson in the history of the businessman, it is that such power cannot be held by the undeserving rich for long. Yet they are always so astonished when the bill collector arrives. Czar Nicholas was apparently as astounded when he and his children were led out to be shot as was Mussolini when he faced hanging by the heels!

To any history student it must appear the silliest illusion a capitalist could harbor that his system of power is permanent. The present structure of capitalism is so new that in the scale of history it might be considered as untried. It is so shaky with structural defects, entrenched weaknesses, and pride in ignoring impartial statistics that even the red fakirs could push it over in nearly half the world and pink fakirs could rock its foundations in the rest.

The American businessman can claim that he is more deserving of protection than those who have been hanged. He did not appear so deserving in 1932! His system does not seem healthy in England and France now. Since 1932 the businessman has not appeared too trustworthy to voters anywhere. The politicos of Europe have been dodging the bill collector in bankruptcy for years. Their necks have been saved from the red ax by American billions. These have been years of "good business."

It is the hope of the businessman that we may never have another depression, but that is only hope. If the capitalists in their shaky world have done anything to prevent it, their wisdom has not become public knowledge. The encouragement of installment buying with "no down payment" is evidence against them. Investment bankers are even now urging states and Authorities to borrow more money in order to get tax free bonds to sell. They have not told us what to expect if our "free world," America and its already bankrupt "allies," enters a period when business really *is* bad.

The strangler fig of the marching debts is still with us, its tentacles reaching ever more deeply into the pockets of investors, management and wage workers everywhere. Demands are now increased by the most astronomical political, private install-ment and mortgage debts. It is a matter of simple arithmetic that we cannot meet all of those de-mands. We can pay the interest as long as the busi-ness boom lasts. Russian economists can tell their followers that it cannot last. That is more than red hope. It is a mathematical certainty that at some point the ever-marching interest demands must overtake the resources of the producers. Newton's Law of Action and Reaction applies as brutally to business as it does to engineering and chemistry.

Our enemies are looking forward eagerly to any collapse of the business cycle sooner or later. That is the hope of barbarians abroad and our own pinks within. Then they hope to take over. As the cycles have followed each other so rhythmically in the past, the reds may be entitled to hope that "the next one" will give them their opportunity. They might even hope that the next one may be one of the worst. America entered the last one with an unshaken dollar and a relatively small debt. After decades of military and political give-away, the dollar now appears a little shaky. Inflation is with us. There will not be so many billions available the next time to "prime the pump." Our debts will be greater than ever.

Then the tax collector and banker, home builder and mortgage broker, and all of those stores now urging us to buy on "easy payments" may be expected to ask for those billions that we owe them. Anybody who owns a government bond may need the money to feed his babies.

In the memory of living Americans there has been no business crisis in which they could not have faith at least in their government's bonds. Our great reservoirs of capital such as banks and insurance companies are largely reservoirs of such paper. The business crisis without parallel in our history could occur if ever the faith of Americans should waver in those promises by their government itself. That crisis already has happened nearly everywhere else. Other countries could look to America for help. America can look only to itself.

It is easy for the reds—or the realistic businessman—to conjure up a disturbing picture of a "businessman's cabinet" struggling to meet a demand for billions with higher taxes in a declining market with all our unemployed and our allies everywhere calling for relief.

In our nation so rich that any rational management could assure us of such abundance as men never have known, the red politico then could charge that every man in a bread line and every baby crying for milk is proof that the business leadership of America has failed.

On that note the case may go to the jury.

The jury might be assisted in its deliberations by atom bombs. As long as the American businessman's production is the chief hope of the world's babies, there is reason to hope that war may remain cold. There could be no stronger invitation to man's hottest war than that he should falter.

It is our American custom to re-elect the politico when business is good—as if he could have much to do with it—but woe to a Hoover or even an Eisenhower if business is bad.

The realistic businessman might recall that even such an eminent businessman as Hoover could not do anything very effective about the last depression. Nor has any other politico ever before or ever since.

The American system does not give any politico much power to make or end depressions. It is an essential of American freedom that no politico shall have such power. It is the American wisdom that all the politicos who ever were given such power failed at the job. The founders of the American system entrusted that power to us. It is largely in the hands of our business leaders. It is dependent on three factors: (1) The available capital free for purchases or investment; (2) the cost of goods and services and their sales organizations; and (3) the national confidence in the minds of 150,000,000 individuals.

In nearly all countries in nearly all of time the politico has persuaded men that free individuals could not be trusted with such power. That is what men decided in Russia in 1917, in Rome long before that, in America and England for a while after 1929, in nearly all countries nearly always.

If the businessman deserves the power that America has given to him, he must know that no politico of whatever party can save him. He must know that he must save himself; and that what must be necessary to save him is nothing less than the most drastic and sweeping reformation and fire-proofing of his capitalist structure.

He must not wait until the fire to attend to the fire-proofing.

He must confront now the cold fact that business cycles and reactions are as inevitable as reactions in chemistry and physics, that the next reaction may confront him with the most threatening fire in the history of the businessman.

If he seeks to retain his power, his money, and that American business freedom in which his fathers could bring forth the economic strength of our nation, he must not permit the next reaction to become the worst. He must not permit the necessary purging of this excess of debt to become a prolonged financial massacre of the innocents who have trusted him.

At some point businessmen must confront the biggest mountains of debt that ever burdened man —matched by the most universal revolt against them.

That is the cold and inescapable challenge which

history is presenting to the business leaders of America.

They ought to know more about how to meet that challenge than any politico can ever know. It is for such wisdom that America has paid them their millions.

If they cannot meet that challenge, the politico must.

12

The Real Issue

In this world war between Left and Right the real issue has somehow become obscured. Especially in America has it been obscured. In this conflict the threat by Kremlin barbarians is only one phase. This may not even be the most threatening phase as the conflict menaces Americans. The real issue is far deeper, broader and almost as old as man himself.

The real issue is whether the productive business of mankind shall be controlled by the non-productive political ruler; or whether that control shall be entrusted to the producers themselves guided by the demands of free consumers.

It is not only the communists who threaten that freedom. There are millions of Americans, many of them passionately sincere in believing they are "liberal" and "progressive," who have their own various programs for taking over that same power.

They find support among all those millions of honest citizens who feel that they cannot trust the businessman.

They put their faith in the non-productive politico; and that same faith is the essential of communism. In Russia the control of producer by politico is absolute. It is the communist faith that men must trust the production and distribution of milk for their babies to the politico who never produced anything himself in the history of the world.

That is the faith not only of communists. It also was the faith of Mussolini, of all political dictators from Caesar to Perón, of the German socialists and Junkers and of Hitler. It was the faith of most of the French revolutionists and it was the faith of Napoleon. It was the faith of all those Latin American revolutionists who established all of the freedoms except one. It was the faith of the Fabian socialists as they undermined the business oligarchy of England. It was the faith of our own New Dealers in their "100 Days."

The antithesis of that faith has been written in the Constitution of the United States. The founders of our American civilization did not trust the political ruler. They imposed upon him checks and balances. In those restrictions on his power the

American producers and businessmen were given the freedom to bring forth the most gigantic production and incomparable wealth in the records of man.

It is this specifically American variety of freedom which has given America most of the steel in the world. It has been the scarcest freedom in history. It is the scarcest freedom in the world now. It is this American variety of freedom which is still considered so controversial, so complex, so questionable, that it is not emphasized in our own schools. Our American civilization has not yet produced the philosopher who could glorify or even justify the greatest producer in history among his own people.

Whether that freedom can survive in America must depend chiefly upon the businessman himself. In that freedom he has won the power of his money. His enemies assert that he cannot be trusted with such power. If the American people believe them, he must lose it.

It is not communism which is the real issue in this world war between Left and Right, especially not in America.

The real issue is the enlightened freedom of the businessman.

Americans will not vote for communism. They may vote against the businessman. They did that for twenty years.

They voted for political control of the businessman—that same political control which ruled in Rome and now rules in Russia—because it seemed to them that the businessman could not be trusted with the power which freedom gave him.

In this war between Left and Right, even the less intelligent voter can easily see that there are two forms of power governing him. There is the power of the man with money who hires and fires him and tells him how much he must pay for coffee. That power in America may seem more important to him than that other power of the political ruler who makes and enforces laws. Even the income tax may seem less important than a rigged market which compels him to pay more for sugar, and whether he has a job or not. It is so easy for the voter to distrust the businessman in the presence of his profit-seeking sins. It is so easy to trust the political ruler who is always so plausible with his eternal promises.

In that war some of our wealthiest men appear to have surrendered.

Like Thyssen embracing Hitler, they hate communism—but they think they can trust their own political rulers to do better. They seem to have overlooked the certain truth that such political rulers can give them no more dependable guarantees than the present guarantee in their Constitution. It is the rock on which all their freedom and power is based. If they permit it to be eaten by termites, then they are loose among all those political currents and confusions perplexing the rest of men. Like the children of the Romanoffs, they can always hope then that the next czar may be better. But they can hardly hope for freedom. It took so long for men to win that.

When they despair at defeating the politico, then, like Thyssen, they join him—and, like Thyssen, may spend their last days writing letters to the editor from cheap boarding houses.

The evidence of such surrender is all around us. It can be seen in the easy acquiescence of business leaders to dictatorship over their workers by some of the most unscrupulous racketeers now become union leaders. It can be seen in their indifference or impotence in opposition to some of the most unscrupulous shysters in government on all levels from local to national. It can be seen in their support of men who refuse to turn their backs on treason.

The power of their money is of no value in upholding freedom.

Their surrender can be seen in the surrender of some of the most powerful newspapers and magazines which they own. They all profess to oppose communism. They fire all their small arms against the Kremlin barbarians. They reserve their biggest guns to shower with infamy those American leaders who fight the threat to our Constitution. They can explode with outrage if such leaders should stoop to fight that threat with the enemy's own weapons.

That threat is a world wide revolt against the businessman's freedom, centered in the most barbarous political despotism in history, dedicated to the first principle that control of the producer by the political ruler shall be absolute. That threat includes and is supplemented by a widespread revolt against the businessman's power in America itself, dedicated to the principle that the businessman must surrender his freedom to that same variety of political domination.

Most Americans have not yet surrendered. Most of America's business leaders, confronted with the clearest evidence of this most insidious and ominous threat to themselves and to the most fundamental principles of America itself, will elect to fight. It is time.

Such an American must look forward to the most savage conflict, internal and external, on paper and perhaps on the battlefield, since the surrender of Cornwallis.

He cannot hope for any profit in victory. If he should be compelled to shatter the enemy capital with atom bombs, he could not hope to win anything from his enemy, not even freedom from the enemy ideas. If he could persuade Congressmen to flush out every last red from our colleges, that would not win the argument on the campus. If a third world war is necessary to "save civilization," he can expect the argument between Left and Right to resume over the atomic ruins.

One of the things he must win is the argument. There is a saying about that which has been echoing around the world. It is something like this: "You can believe what you like about communism, but you can't beat a communist in an argument." The American businessman has hardly even tried to win the argument. Boiling the communist argument to its essentials, the residue is that many businessmen have been bad. The answer is so easy. It is that the political control the Russians offer is always so much worse. All government planning is always at the expense of the people's plans. The politico must tax us out of our money for his plans. He does not risk his own money. He risks ours. Most of us are sure to be more careful in risking our own money than he is. Most of us are producers. The red planner never is. He is the same politico who has been seeking the power of our money ever since the first racketeer wielded the first club on his fellow man. We must produce something to get such power. He never does. He seeks that power by swinging his club over our heads, by force, taxes or some other threat.

13

Battle Plan

            When the business leaders of America elect to fight, they may call for a positive program. They will probably call for the facts, based on research. Any such research must penetrate unexplored regions. There can be few precedents of value in history for such a conflict. The reason is simple. There never has been such a country as the United States. There never has been any country in which such economic freedom has so long prevailed. There never has been such a demonstration of the productive power of that freedom. There never has been in American history such a universal threat to that freedom. The American leaders who enter that fight can have no more useful precedents to guide them than Washington and Jefferson had. They must make their own.

The precedents in history are nearly all negative.

They can tell us what not to do. They can be found in the downfall of all those other states where the businessman won some such freedom from the political ruler in the past. There are not many of them—the chief ones were Carthage and Corinth, Venice and Florence, Lubeck and England—and in none of them was this freedom of the producer so complete. There is one simple lesson from all of them. That is that the businessman was too busy making profits to safeguard his freedom to make them. His downfall always came after his lust for profits caused him to lose the respect of his own people.

The business burghers of Germany and Holland lost their freedom when they sold cannons to the enemy barons. The heirs of the British business oligarchy have been doing that in China.

If the American business leader seeks precedents in his own brief history, he can find a glorious chapter in 1776. It is a thin chapter. American businessmen have not risen to such political heights since. They have had a strenuous and constant struggle to retain the support of their own people. The exploits of their "robber barons" cost them that support in the first big invasion of their freedom in 1933.

THE BUSINESSMAN MUST SAVE HIMSELF

Any business leader who hopes that this greatest of business civilizations may survive must base his hopes first of all on the respect, confidence and support of the American people. Without that there can be no hope. He must regain and keep that confidence. To do that he must justify it. There is no other way.

If his power is in his money, the people have the same right to demand an honest business statesmanship in the use of that power as they demand from the political power of the men they elect to office. The first essential in such business statesmanship is that it must be based on rigorous honesty to the interests of the people as a whole.

Whenever the small businessman misuses the power of his money to win an unfair profit with a sharp deal, he can argue that he has merely won a battle with an enemy in the struggle for existence. It is a weak argument. He has disgraced himself in a small way and earned the hate of the victim for himself and probably his class.

There is no such defense available to the big businessman. He may not regard the public as an enemy to be bamboozled. His power is so large that it becomes a matter of the public health. He may not hope to put over sharp deals on the public and long survive. It is too easy for the citizens to take away his power. They may not understand the complexities of the deal whereby they have been swindled. They may not understand the intricacies of the latest Federal Reserve move or the workings of the tariff. But they can demand that the politico take over when it appears that they always get the worst of things. That is what they have been doing.

The enlightened business leader must look to the American public as a prisoner accused of crime must look to the jury which has powers over him of life and death. If he is to survive, it must be because he can win and hold the confidence and support of that public. Such confidence and support cannot be won in terms of profit per share.

His own power demands from him a positive and intensely active statesmanship that must go far beyond profits, and the winning of votes in a political party convention. That statesmanship must extend to such diverse fields as foreign affairs, education, and labor relations.

It is in those fields that he must face the heaviest enemy guns and expect the most ferocious and fanatical resistance. A brief look at those battlefields reveals a pitiful story of the businessman's weakness, inertia and surrenders.

The businessman has made big profits from his foreign policies. It was our financial leaders themselves who made huge foreign loans which they must have known could not be paid. Their profits were made at the expense of bond buyers who trusted them.

Our government took over where private financiers left off. It poured out billions. It gave up the pretense that they were loans. They were now outright gifts—to save us from those foreign menaces which American policies did so much to create. The supplications of the foreign politico for gifts to save him and us now have been replaced with a barely veiled blackmail—"give us billions or we must go red."

In nearly all of those foreign lands where so many men lack enough to eat, there are inviting vacuums for American development capital. There are big and honest chances for profitable investments if some way could be found to keep the foreign politico's itchy fingers out of them. To justify any such risk of American sweat, there are some essential requisites. One of them is that such a loan would develop enough production to permit repayment. Another is that such repayment should not be prevented by our own tariffs. A third might be that such development would help to feed the citizens of the country involved, not merely to fatten the bank accounts of the political crowd that gets the loan.

Of the hundreds of billions of American dollars poured out in recent years, few have been spent with such elemental common sense. Most of them have been wasted in war. Most of the remainder have been spent to save foreign citizens from the consequences of their own sins. Many billions have been spent merely to balance foreign budgets; that is, to uphold the politico who could bamboozle us into giving him our money.

The American business leader who hopes to win the confidence of his people cannot surrender to such moral turpitude. He must be prepared to reject with contempt the profits that are offered on such deals. If such loans must be made from his people's sweat, he must be prepared to surrender something so that they can be repaid. He can justify an outright gift of military help to a friend threatened with military attack. He cannot justify any surrender to blackmail.

The American leader who elects to fight such blackmail must be prepared to face all the enemy guns. He will be threatened with disaster at once. He can expect to be pilloried abroad and confront at home all the smears by all those Americans who have surrendered. He may lack the courage to risk the fate of Forrestal. Then he must face another risk. That is the risk of cataclysm at home and abroad when the gifts are exhausted.

It is an ideological war which the businessman must fight, the sort of war that he has been accustomed to leave to such lookers-on as writers, professors, and clergymen. To justify his existence he must win the argument; but so many of those lookers-on are against him. It is a war which must be fought everywhere that men argue, from the corner barber shop to the international conference, from the elementary school room to the United States Senate, from the labor union hall to those military outposts where his defenders have been losing their lives. At stake are his reasons for existence. At stake are the freedom of producer and consumer which makes the existence of the free businessman possible. That freedom is an essential, perhaps even the most important essential, in his Constitution. It is certainly the essential difference between the American business civilization and nearly all other democracies.

The importance of that freedom is hardly even taught in American schools. It is hardly even discussed until the American student reaches the college classes in economics, political science, sociology —which have been a chief target in the red onslaught. Such has been the inertia of the businessman that those classrooms may yet see the decisive battle in his fight for existence.

Over the last century the businessman has been subtly trying to take over control of American colleges. His gifts to education permitted him to replace the clergyman on the board of trustees. He has given American schools little leadership. His control has been limited to a heavy frowning upon any criticism of business, whether honest or not.

Such torpid supervision could not be expected to win enthusiastic support from intellectuals. It found its expression when "socialistic" professors were fired. The reaction of the campus found one expression in Hubert Park Beck's *Men Who Control Our*

Universities. It found a more threatening expression after 1929. That disgrace left him wide open to the red attack on the campus. His own son might learn that the old man was not only a superannuated Babbitt but maybe also an anti-social rascal.

When the business leader calls for a positive program based on research, he may expect little help from the past. The research may be more fruitful if it is directed at what is going on now. It is the political ruler who can try to find precedents to justify him in that past. The business leader must find his precedents in the relatively brief history of business freedom.

He can assert that it is that specific variety of freedom which has given to America the wealth to build the biggest universities. He might establish a precedent by asserting that the importance of that specific freedom should be given more emphasis in the universities. He might direct careful research to those classes on political science and economics, sociology and teaching, which have been one of his weakest points under the heaviest attack from his enemies. He might demand that the importance of that specific freedom should be emphasized in all schools. The teachers have been telling the children about all the other freedoms—of press and religion and speech—but not that one. The business leader might establish a precedent when he asks the leaders of the National Education Association: why not? Then he might be prepared for the biggest uproar in the history of American education.

His positive program must demand the most intensive research into his relations with what is called "labor."

He can tell American workers that he pays them the highest wages for the shortest hours ever heard of in the world. It might seem to him that argument ought to be conclusive. It has not been enough. It has not won labor peace. The master-and-servant relationship remains. The producer is still an inferior fellow. Instead of seeking protection from a feudal lord, he seeks it now from a union dictator. American freedom has given to the American worker his automobile. It has not yet given him much pride in his work.

Any positive program for the businessman must demand the most intensive research into that master-and-servant relationship. Of course such research has been going on. It has brought forth various hopeful profit-sharing plans. It is often so easy for the red enemy to point out that the boss continues to reserve the lion's share of the profits for himself. It seems possible that a fair formula already has been devised for use in certain factories and industries. These new "incentive management" programs now appear to be a success.

The employer and the worker himself must see that any plan to succeed must be really honest, honest to him and also honest to the investor, management and consumer. The business leader can hardly hope for much success from any program that offers less. Any incentive management program calls on the worker for all of his intelligence and skill to give his best as a member of the team, with honest incentive and pride of achievement in the incredible possible increases in production.

In the final analysis, the workers want an increase in their standard of living with security and reasonable work conditions. For these things wage disputes and wasteful strikes are primarily waged. May it be that these ends can best be hastened not by new legislation but by research in the fields of physics, chemistry and metallurgy, including inventions, discoveries and new processes? In addition to what Atomic Energy may do for mankind, if properly used, I have in mind the following ten thoughts:

(1) New metals and alloys which are lighter, stronger and cheaper than any now known.

(2) Indestructible plastics in all colors which can be used for better clothing and homes—thus eliminating wear and maintenance.

(3) New uses for electronics, not only in production and distribution but for the protection of humans and crops against ever increasing pests and insects. Robot brain machines have marvelous possibilities.

(4) Photosynthesis studies whereby the air, light, water and minerals now used by the plants can be combined directly into food, thus eliminating agricultural drudgery. In this connection we must not forget artificial insemination.

(5) Capturing for useful purposes the supersonic and other unused waves which are now entering our homes like radio waves—but not being used.

(6) The use of solar radiation for free heat in winter, free air conditioning in summer, hot water and other household benefits throughout the year.

(7) The discovery of new miracle drugs which

will eliminate all infectious diseases and assure good health and long life to all who will live properly.

(8) A revolution of our educational system which will make citizens truly intelligent, useful and happy—perhaps greatly reducing the incidence of mental diseases.

(9) Discovering how the firefly manufactures cold light and using the secret for many purposes from flash lights to general illumination.

(10) Securing from the sea its unlimited and constantly increasing supply of food, minerals and power.

In addition to the above, there are the possibilities of finding a partial insulator against gravity. This could greatly reduce weight which is the greatest factor in the cost of living.

These are the studies which Associations of Manufacturers might be making and generally encouraging instead of fighting labor along present lines. If one half of what is now lost by employers through strikes were used for cooperative research along the above and other lines, their workers would constantly be given higher wages, more security and better working conditions. From such research all parties—stockholders, employees and consumers —would benefit as no price increases might be necessary.

Some will complain that such new discoveries and inventions would reduce the demands for labor. It is true that in some instances labor demands would be less; but we all would have more leisure time along with a higher standard of living. Furthermore, some of the goals would develop entirely new industries which would offer far more and greater opportunities than the sicknesses, maintenance losses and "horse and buggy" customs of today.

In such fields of research, American genius continues at work on those innovations which have made America so different from all police states. All of them depend upon one first essential. That is political freedom. Their progress must also depend on that form of government which comes from business leadership. Their plans and programs must falter if that leadership should fail in depression.

It is in this world of investments and profits, ticker tape and paper promises, the headquarters of capitalism itself facing its greatest task, that such research may be most profitable. It is to their business leaders that Americans must look for hope that the worst evils of the business cycle may be averted, that its hardships may be minimized. If the business leadership should fail, it must not be for lack of evidence and warnings of its errors. It will not be for lack of opportunities for new industries and processes calling for development to raise the standards of living to new high levels.

To Lenin has been attributed the dictum that "the surest way to destroy the capitalist system is to debauch its currency." The late Lord Keynes commented: "Lenin was certainly right. The process engages all the hidden forces of economic law on the side of destruction, and does it in a manner which not one man in a million is able to diagnose." It is America's financial leaders who should be best able to diagnose it.

If that leadership is to survive its greatest test, it must be because those business leaders have had the wisdom and courage to do what their forebears in all those fallen business freedoms of the past have failed to do.

They must justify their leadership with a program of positive statesmanship based on one essential—a rigorous honesty to the interests of the

American people whose support they must have to survive. That program must call for nothing less than a Business Reformation.

The American Business Reformation can be expected to succeed if it is based on a new dedication to the principles of freedom and business integrity which are implicit in the Constitution.

It will recognize that the realities of power in America are in two forms—the power of the political ruler and what remains of the power of free business leadership.

It will demand and enforce a new integrity and statesmanship in the use of the power of money. It will reject and prosecute unfair profit-making which abuses the confidence in business of their people. It will give active assistance to the political branch in enforcing business honesty as rigorous as business leaders demand from themselves on the floor of the New York Stock Exchange—and for the same reason—because only integrity permits the Exchange to survive.

It will demand that the political ruler perform an honest job at what is the first duty of the political ruler in all times and places—to prevent men from robbing each other. It will demand first of all that the political ruler, in the performance of that first duty, shall drive out of the business world those pirates and practices which have disgraced business —and the enlightened business leader will actively assist the political ruler in doing it.

If the business leaders of America can find it in themselves to undertake a positive program based on those essentials, they might hope to find the details easier in the sunlight of the new directions.

They can then be confident of an overwhelming support of their people in which threats to business might be expected to wither. They could look forward to a new era of production and prosperity in a finer civilization.

In the pages of history, business leaders then could look the image of George Washington in the face and say:

"I had almost as hard a fight as you had. Your Constitution is safe."

14

America Can Be Saved

The businessman is still supposed to possess great wisdom. He is the only one of us with wisdom enough to turn mountains into plowshares. He ought to know more about the cause and cure of depressions than any politico. To save his own life and the lives of his family he should take a much greater interest in both economic and moral problems.

It has not been necessary here to differentiate between the farmer and manufacturer who organize production, the banker and broker who finance production, the merchant who distributes it, and the consumer who buys it. They are all "businessmen." Together they have created the economic grandeur of the United States. Together they have given the western world a richer life than men have ever known. Together they have given us the wars, the depressions, the booms and the business mistakes which now confront us.

If men can be relieved of the agonies of widespread poverty suffered in depressions in the midst of abundance, the banker should know better than any politico how to do it. If his wisdom is not overestimated, he might be able to reduce those mountains of debt which now threaten our civilization without precipitating a prolonged financial disaster for the rest of us. America has given him another chance.

America now retains the vast powers of its money. We may have the wisdom to avert or minimize the hardships of the next depression. We may have learned that to retain such power we must use it as responsible citizens. We may have learned that we must do a more responsible job of the business of farming, manufacturing, banking, advertising, merchandising and buying, with greater restraint and wisdom. If American businessmen could be given such wisdom, they might regain the public confidence which they must have to survive.

They could then win their war for survival with a *Business Reformation* which could give us the greatest abundance known in all the history of man.

This would mean that the American businessman and his wage workers would have the wits to lead themselves in the fight for business integrity which is implicit in their own Constitution. The genuine freedom of honest and competitive work is the real basis for lasting prosperity and power.

It would mean that he would have sense enough to renounce his own mistakes as a matter of business policy because they are not worth what they cost. He would demand that the market place should be an honest place where honest businessmen and their employees could perform their honest job of developing the cheapest possible distribution to bring forth the greatest possible production. He would lead the fight to drive out of the market place the worst thieves as English bankers two centuries before drove pirates from the seas,—because it paid.

He would fight any rigging of the stock market or the labor market and every other market as a swindle. He would take his own honest chances with the law of supply and demand, which is his job. That means he would actually take the lead in demanding the enforcement of anti-monopoly laws applied to both capital and labor. He would join his own victims in demanding the end of both "price and wage agreements," tariff politics, scarcity schemes, phony installment booms which he knows must collapse in a depression, instead of riding along with all these in the hopes he would get out before the collapse.

He would fight to make his market place honest. He would join the police in fighting racketeers, whether business or labor leaders. He knows them so much better than the police do. He would fight to save himself and his job with the simplest and strongest strategy,—by doing a better job as a better businessman, guided by research and impartial statistics.

The great lions of the market place have the power to save themselves with such a Reformation. Little business will then take courage when they hear an American banker saying:

"I will never lend a dollar to your corporation until you announce that you will never ask a Congressman for an unjust favor.

"I will throw overboard every bond and share I own in your company the moment you make another illegal price agreement.

"There never will be another dime for your law school until you quit turning young Americans into corrupt practitioners. I have a million for any school or publisher who can teach the truth about business.

"I haven't a dime for the Democratic Party until you turn your back to traitors and shysters; I haven't a nickel for the Republican Party until you quit killing the goose which has laid your own golden eggs.

"Both parties have been destroying competition in America with trade, agricultural and labor subsidies. When they are wide awake enough to know they are committing suicide, they can come and see me.

"Finally, I am tired of hearing you complain that your workers and their leaders are 'no good!' It is up to you to help them become good and recognize that their faults may be due to you and your fathers."

In our times it may be impossible for bankers to talk like that. Perhaps it would not be fair to the stockholders. There was a time when it was different. That was when American bankers were risking their money and their lives to finance Valley Forge. It was when one of the richest Americans was writing the Constitution which has made the miracle of American business possible. It was when the richest man of them all was crossing the Delaware. Such businessmen would save us now.

Epilogue

The University of Chicago has published an important book known as *The Short Bible*. It gives an impartial collection of the experiences of the past 3500 years which our Bible covers. Among other features, the sixty-six books of our Bible are arranged, in this University of Chicago publication, chronologically,—that is, in the order of the dates when these different books were written.

The earliest book of the Old Testament is not *Genesis*, but rather *Micah* which makes this appeal:

"O, Man, what is good; what does the Lord require of Thee but to do justice, to love mercy and to walk humbly with thy God."

In a few words this is the substance of the Gospel which Jesus preached some centuries later.

To the above, the present day businessman can

in substance reply: "According to the above Chicago University publication, the oldest book in the New Testament is not *St. Matthew*, but rather *Thessalonians*. By referring to the latest Revised Standard Version, we find the 10th verse of the third chapter of *Thessalonians* reads as follows:

"We give you this command; If anyone will not work let him not eat."

Perhaps this apparent conflict in doctrine is in part responsible for the mess in which the businessman finds himself today. If so, economists, preachers, politicos and all the rest of us should seek a fair coalescence of the above two commands. Only a spiritual awakening will give us the best answers to all social and economic problems.

Set in Linotype Caledonia
Format by Edwin H. Kaplin
Manufactured by The Haddon Craftsmen, Inc.
Published by HARPER & BROTHERS, New York